A Robbie Reader

MIGUEL CABRERA

Joanne Mattern

Mitchell Lane
PUBLISHERS

P.O. Box 196
Hockessin, Delaware 19707
Visit us on the web: www.mitchelllane.com
Comments? Email us: mitchelllane@mitchelllane.com

Printing 1 2 3 4 5 6 7 8 9

A Robbie Reader Biography

Abigail Breslin
Adrian Peterson
Albert Einstein
Albert Pujols
Aly and AJ
Andrew Luck
AnnaSophia Robb
Ashley Tisdale
Brenda Song
Brittany Murphy
Buster Posey
Charles Schulz
Chris Johnson
Cliff Lee
Dale Earnhardt Jr.
David Archuleta
Demi Lovato
Donovan McNabb
Drake Bell & Josh Peck
Dr. Seuss
Dwayne "The Rock" Johnson
Dwyane Wade
Dylan & Cole Sprouse
Emily Osment
Hilary Duff
Jamie Lynn Spears
Jennette McCurdy
Jesse McCartney
Jimmie Johnson
Joe Flacco
Jonas Brothers
Keke Palmer
Larry Fitzgerald
LeBron James
Mia Hamm
Miguel Cabrera
Miley Cyrus
Miranda Cosgrove
Philo Farnsworth
Raven-Symoné
Robert Griffin III
Roy Halladay
Shaquille O'Neal
Story of Harley-Davidson
Sue Bird
Syd Hoff
Tiki Barber
Tim Lincecum
Tom Brady
Tony Hawk
Troy Polamalu
Victor Cruz
Victoria Justice

Library of Congress Cataloging-in-Publication Data
Mattern, Joanne, 1963- author.
Miguel Cabrera / by Joanne Mattern.
pages cm. — (A Robbie reader)
Includes bibliographical references and index.
ISBN 978-1-61228-457-6 (library bound)
1. Cabrera, Miguel, 1983- —Juvenile literature. 2. Baseball players—Venezuela—Biography—Juvenile literature. I. Title.
GV865.C25M38 2014
796.357092—dc23
[B]

2013023058

eBook ISBN: 9781612285153

ABOUT THE AUTHOR: Joanne Mattern has written many nonfiction books for children. Previous biographies for Mitchell Lane include *Benny Goodman, Count Basie, One Direction, Jennifer Hudson, The Jonas Brothers, Ludacris*, and *Selena*. Joanne lives with her husband, four children, and several pets in New York State.

PUBLISHER'S NOTE: The following story has been thoroughly researched and to the best of our knowledge represents a true story. While every possible effort has been made to ensure accuracy, the publisher will not assume liability for damages caused by inaccuracies in the data, and makes no warranty on the accuracy of the information contained herein. This story has not been authorized or endorsed by Miguel Cabrera.

PLB

TABLE OF CONTENTS

Words in **bold** type can be found in the glossary.

Miguel Cabrera hits a two-run home run in the first inning of Game 4 of the 2003 World Series against the New York Yankees.

CHAPTER ONE

No Fear

It was the 2003 World Series. The Florida Marlins were playing against the New York Yankees. Few people thought the Marlins had a chance against the powerful New York team. The Yankees had won more World Series than any other team in baseball. But the Marlins were up to the challenge. So was their **rookie** outfielder, Miguel Cabrera.

When Game 4 started, the Yankees were up two games to one. In the first inning of Game 4, Cabrera faced Yankees pitcher Roger Clemens. Clemens was one of the best pitchers in the game. The big pitcher had a strong fastball that scared some players. Cabrera had never faced Clemens before. He stepped up to the plate, squared his bat, and waited for the first pitch.

Clemens hurled a fastball at 92 miles an hour. The ball whizzed by Cabrera's chin like a warning. Cabrera turned toward the pitcher and glared at him. Then he got ready for the next pitch.

Cabrera ran the count to two strikes, two balls, and two fouls. Finally, Clemens threw his seventh pitch at the young outfielder. Cabrera swung and hit the ball hard. It sailed over the right-field wall. Home run!

Cabrera's home run gave the Marlins a 2-0 lead. The Marlins ended up winning the game 4-3 and tying the series at two games apiece. After that, the Yankees didn't have a chance. A few days later, the Marlins won the World Series four games to two. It was only the second time the Marlins had won the World Series.

Cabrera talks with New York Yankees' Ruben Sierra (left) and other players during practice before Game 5 of the 2003 World Series. The Marlins defeated the Yankees 6-4 to take a 3-2 series lead.

Miguel Cabrera's courage at the plate that night impressed everyone. According to Sam Alipour with *ESPN The Magazine*, his teammate Mike Redmond said, "This kid isn't afraid of anything." The moment still makes Redmond smile. Later, Alipour asked Cabrera if he was afraid of Clemens. Cabrera had a simple answer to that question: "Naw." When it comes to baseball, very little scares Miguel Cabrera.

Miguel Cabrera was only 16 when the Florida Marlins signed him to a minor-league contract. Cabrera sat quietly at an August 4, 1999, press conference announcing the decision.

Born into Baseball

Jose Miguel Cabrera was born on April 18, 1983. He was born in Maracay, Venezuela. His parents were Miguel and Gregoria. He also had a younger sister named Ruth. The Cabrera family lived in a tiny house in a poor neighborhood called La Pedrera.

Miguel's father was a player in the **amateur** baseball leagues in Venezuela. He hoped to play **professional** baseball, but never made it. Instead, he ran an auto repair shop.

Miguel's mother was a star shortstop for the Venezuelan national softball team. Gregoria's brother, David Torres, was also a baseball star in Venezuela. Later he played with the St. Louis Cardinals' **minor league** teams. However, he never made it to the **major leagues** and moved back to Maracay.

Baseball was a huge part of Miguel's life. When he was little, he often played in the dugout during his mother's softball practices. He also played for hours with his father and his uncle. The Cabrera home was right next to the baseball field in Maracay. Little Miguel often hopped over the stadium's fence to watch games and play. Later, the stadium in Maracay was named David Torres Stadium after Miguel's uncle.

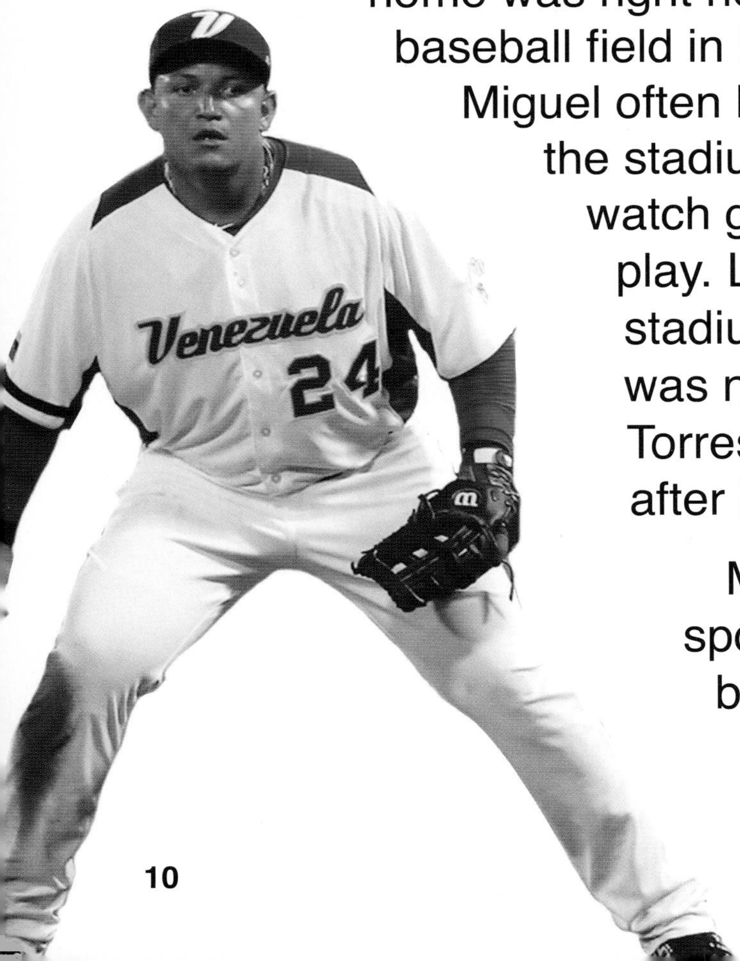

Miguel loved all sports, but baseball was number one. When he was about 12 years old, Miguel told his family that he wanted to play professional baseball. His father and uncle decided it was too soon to start training. Miguel still had many years to change his mind. His family encouraged him to keep getting good grades in school if he wanted to play. Miguel did stay in school, but he could not stop thinking about baseball.

By the time Miguel was 14 years old, his uncle David Torres could see that he was ready. He planned to begin his training in January 1998. Sadly, Torres died of a heart attack in 1997, just before the new year. "That was one of the factors that helped me to keep pushing ahead," Miguel later told the *Sun Sentinel*. "In January, we were going to start working. Those are things you have to deal with in life."

Miguel's father began working less so he could coach his son. It wasn't long before **scouts** from American teams were traveling to Maracay to see the young baseball star.

Cabrera was still a teenager when he put on a Marlins uniform and headed to the United States to play professional baseball.

Coming to America

By the time he was fifteen years old, Miguel Cabrera had gotten the attention of several major league baseball teams. Scouts were sent down to Maracay to see him. Cabrera's favorite player was Alex Gonzalez, a shortstop for the Florida Marlins at the time. So he was excited when a Marlins scout named Louie Eljaua came to see him in 1998. Eljaua was impressed by Cabrera's talent. The teenager had a powerful swing that produced many hits. He was also a great fielder and had a strong throwing arm. Eljaua told the Marlins they should sign Cabrera.

Teams from all over the United States tried to sign Cabrera. The Dodgers and the Yankees offered more than two million dollars. But Cabrera's heart was with the Florida Marlins. He and his family were happy with the way that the Marlins worked with young Latino players. They knew the team would take care of him. In July 1999, 16-year-old Cabrera signed a **contract** to play with the Florida Marlins for $1.8 million.

Cabrera traveled to Florida in 2000. He was sent to a minor league team where he did very well in his first season. He played for different Marlins minor league teams for the next four seasons. He continued to play well and impress everyone with his skills.

Cabrera found life off the field harder than life playing baseball. He did not speak any English when he first came to Florida. Later he told reporter Sam Alipour with *ESPN The Magazine*, "You can't do anything because you don't go places where you have to speak. You go to eat, you eat the same thing: Burger King."

Cabrera knew he had to learn English if he wanted to feel comfortable in the United States. So he signed up for English classes. Then a teammate suggested he read the newspapers. Reading newspapers helped a lot. "People make fun of me because they say I see only the pictures," Cabrera told Alipour, "but I learn to see the words they say."

In time, Cabrera's English got much better, but he still worries he will not be understood. He shared with Alipour, "If I say something wrong, it's a big thing on Twitter."

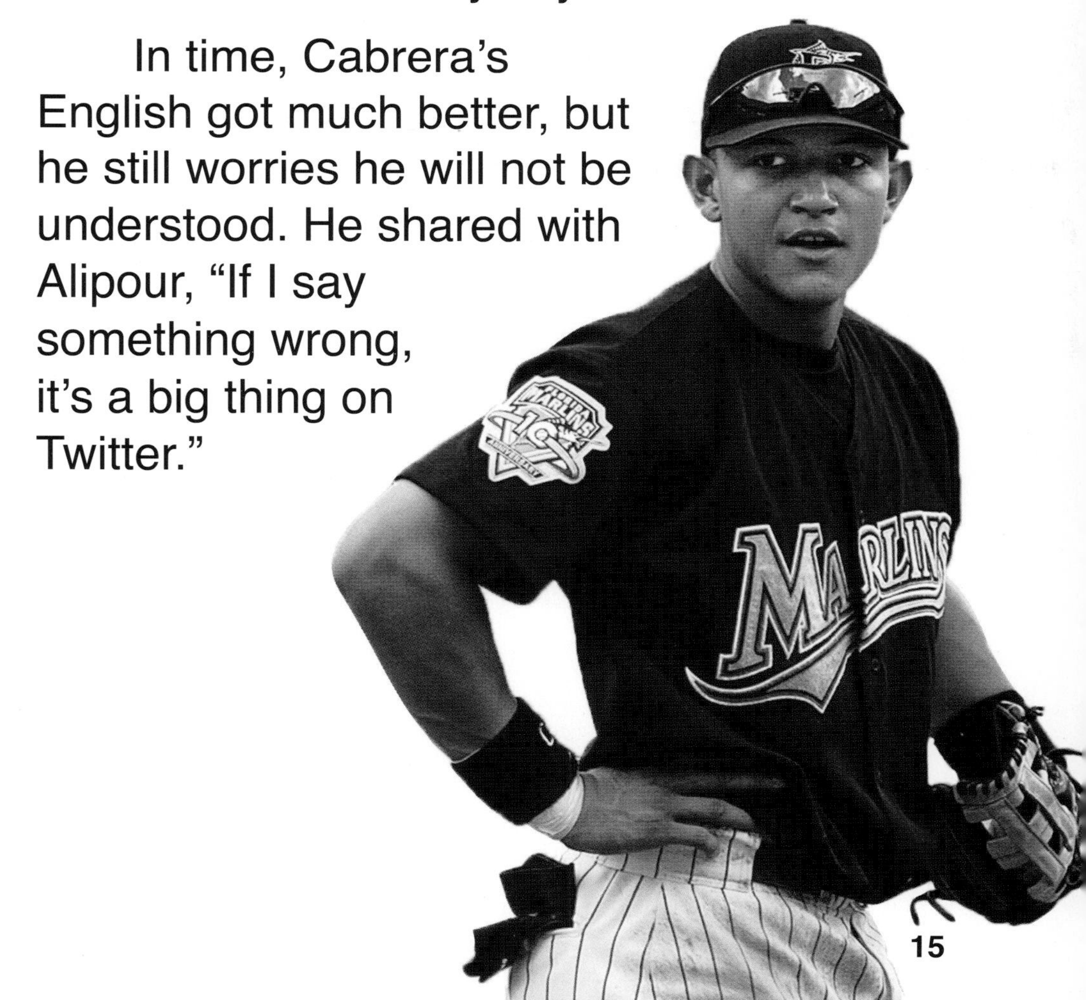

Third baseman Miguel Cabrera throws the ball in a game against the San Francisco Giants during a National League Division Series game.

Big Leagues, Big Star

Cabrera started the 2002 season playing for the Jupiter Hammerheads. This was one of the Marlins' top minor league teams. A manager suggested that Cabrera switch from shortstop to third base. Cabrera loved his new position, and he continued to play at third base in 2003. Everyone expected he would spend another year in the minor leagues. But the Marlins were not doing well. They needed some new talent. On June 20, 2003, 20-year-old Cabrera was called up to the big leagues. Because the Marlins already had a strong third baseman, Cabrera played left field.

Cabrera slides into home base with a winning run in the ninth inning in a game against the Philadelphia Phillies on July 27, 2003.

With Cabrera's help, the Marlins began to win. They made the playoffs as a **wild-card team**. Cabrera also began to play games at third base. He was named the National League Rookie of the Month in July and September. That fall, the Marlins won the World Series.

During the All-Star break in 2003, Miguel Cabrera made a big change in his personal life. He married his high school sweetheart, Rosangel. In 2005, the couple had their first child. They named their new daughter Rosangel after her mother, but she is usually called Brisel. The Cabreras had another daughter, Isabella, in 2010, and a son, Christopher, in 2011.

Cabrera continued to star for the Marlins for the next few years. Then, in December 2007, the Marlins traded Cabrera to the Detroit Tigers. He was shocked and hurt. Cabrera faced another big change when he joined the Tigers. The team's manager, Jim Leyland, switched him to first base.

Despite his feelings, Cabrera quickly felt right at home with his new team. During his first season with the Tigers, he led the American League with 37 homers. He played well for the next few seasons.

In 2011, the Tigers made it into the playoffs. Their first

On April 23, 2011, Cabrera received the 2010 Louisville Slugger Silver Slugger Award. Detroit Tigers vice president and assistant general manager Al Avila presented the award to Cabrera.

Cabrera walks off the field with his family after Game 4 of the American League Championship Series against the New York Yankees on October 18, 2012. Cabrera says his family is the most important thing in his life.

opponent was the New York Yankees. The Tigers won the series in five games and went on to the American League Championships. There, the Tigers faced the Texas Rangers. Detroit played well, but the Rangers ended up winning the championship and a place in the World Series.

The Tigers decided to make some changes after that season. The next few years would be interesting ones for Cabrera and his team.

During a game against the Kansas City Royals, a fan shows her support for Cabrera and the Tigers with a homemade sign. The Tigers defeated the Royals 5-4.

Trouble and Triumph

Although Cabrera was a success on the field, he also faced serious personal problems. In 2009, he and his wife got into a fight and the police were called. Cabrera's **blood alcohol level** was very high. He was embarrassed, especially when he had to face his team. The Tigers' general manager, Dave Dombrowski, told reporters that Cabrera was eager to get help. Cabrera went to **counseling** and did well for a while.

Then, in 2011, Cabrera got into an argument at a Florida restaurant. Later that night, police found Cabrera in his car on the side of the road. Cabrera was drinking and put up a fight when the police tried to arrest him. Once again, Cabrera went to counseling. Since then, he has stopped drinking. "It was a wake-up call," Cabrera told *ESPN The Magazine*. "I'm able to be strong and say no."

Cabrera was back on track in 2012. That year, the Tigers signed Prince Fielder to play first base. Once again, Cabrera moved back to third base. He worked hard to be the best at this position. During spring training, Cabrera stayed after practice to catch ground balls. His teammates and Tigers fans appreciated his hard work. "That kind of **sacrifice** for the good of the team rubs people in a good way, especially in a . . . town like Detroit," one fan told *ESPN The Magazine*.

Cabrera had a great season in 2012. He was named Most Valuable Player of the American League. Cabrera scored 44 home runs and 139 **RBIs**. He ended the season with a .330 batting average. He was at the top of the American League in all three categories, earning him baseball's

Triple Crown. It was the first time a player had won the Triple Crown since 1967. Cabrera received another honor in 2013 when he was named the best player in baseball by the popular ESPN television show, *Baseball Tonight*.

Hall of Famer Frank Robinson presents the Triple Crown award to Miguel Cabrera on October 27, 2012.

CHAPTER FIVE

In 2012, Cabrera started the Miguel Cabrera Foundation to help children find success through sports and community activities.

Cabrera is a hero on the field, and he does his best to be a hero off the field as well. He especially loves working with children. Cabrera has helped several charities, including Keeping Kids in the Game and Tigers Dreams Come True. Cabrera has also worked with children in Baseball Fantasy Camp for Kids.

In 2012, Cabrera decided to start his own **foundation** to help children. The Miguel Cabrera Foundation helps kids and their families succeed using baseball as a guide. The foundation creates youth development programs, community ballparks, and youth leadership academies.

Miguel Cabrera is a talented player who is sure to be in the National Baseball Hall of Fame someday. Baseball is important to him, but so is helping others and being with his family. "For me, family is the most **fundamental** thing in the world," Cabrera told MLB.com. "I am here because I have had the support of my family and my wife all the time. . . you always need your family and it does not matter how young or old you are."

CAREER STATISTICS

Year	Team	G	PA	AB	R	H	2B	3B	HR	RBI	SB	CS	BB	SO	BA	OBP
2003	Florida Marlins	87	346	314	39	84	21	3	12	62	0	2	25	84	.268	.325
2004	Florida Marlins	160	685	603	101	177	31	1	33	112	5	2	68	148	.294	.366
2005	Florida Marlins	158	685	613	106	198	43	2	33	116	1	0	64	125	.323	.385
2006	Florida Marlins	158	676	576	112	195	50	2	26	114	9	6	86	108	.339	.430
2007	Florida Marlins	157	680	588	91	188	38	2	34	119	2	1	79	127	.320	.401
2008	Detroit Tigers	160	684	616	85	180	36	2	**37**	127	1	0	56	126	.292	.349
2009	Detroit Tigers	160	685	611	96	198	34	0	34	103	6	2	68	107	.324	.396
2010	Detroit Tigers	150	648	548	111	180	45	1	38	**126**	3	3	89	95	.328	**.420**
2011	Detroit Tigers	**161**	688	572	111	197	**48**	0	30	105	1	1	108	89	**.344**	**.448**
2012	Detroit Tigers	161	697	622	109	205	40	0	44	**139**	1	1	66	98	**.330**	.393
As of 8/26/13	Detroit Tigers	116	522	444	**89**	**160**	24	1	40	**120**	3	0	72	75	**.360**	**.452**

G–Games Played
PA–Plate Apperances
AB–At Bats
R–Runs Scored
H–Hits
2B–Doubles
3B–Triples
HR–Home Runs
RBI–Runs Batted In
SB–Stolen Bases
CS–Caught Stealing
BB–Bases on Balls
SO–Strikeouts
BA–Batting Average
OBP–On Base Percentage

PHOTO CREDITS: Cover, pp. 1, 20, 22–Mark Cunningham/MLB Photos via Getty Images; pp. 4, 16–Eliot J. Schechter/Getty Images; p. 7–Mike Albans/NY Daily News Achive via Getty Images; p. 8–AP Photo/Tony Gutierrez, File; p. 10–Stephen Dunn/Getty Images; p. 12–Andy Lyons/Getty Images; p. 18–AP Photo/Richard Patterson; p. 21–Leon Halip/Getty Images; p. 25–Ron Vesely/MLB Photos via Getty Images; p. 26–Miguel Cabrera Foundation; pp. 27, 29–Keith Allison/cc-by-sa. Every effort has been made to locate all copyright holders of material used in this book. If any errors or omissions have occurred, corrections will be made in future editions of this book.

CHRONOLOGY

1983 Miguel Cabrera is born on April 18.

1998 Tries out for the Florida Marlins.

1999 Signs a $1.8 million contract with the Marlins.

2000 Makes his first appearance in the minor leagues.

2003 Called up to the major leagues where he helps the Marlins win the World Series. Marries his high school sweetheart, Rosangel.

2005 First child is born, named Rosangel.

2007 Traded to the Detroit Tigers.

2010 Daughter Isabella is born.

2011 Son Christopher is born.

2012 Named the American League's Most Valuable Player and wins the Triple Crown. Forms the Miguel Cabrera Foundation.

2013 Has one of his best seasons and is one of the stars of the All-Star Game in July.

FIND OUT MORE

Books and Magazines

Detroit Free Press. *Days of Roar! From Miguel Cabrera's Triple Crown to a Dynasty in the Making!* Chicago: Triumph Books, 2013.

Fishman, Jon M. *Miguel Cabrera*. Minneapolis, MN: Lerner, 2013.

Repanich, Jeremy. "Miguel Cabrera: How He Won the Triple Crown." *Sports Illustrated Kids*, April 12, 2013. http://www.sikids.com/blogs/2013/04/12/miguel-cabrera-how-he-won-the-triple-crown

Works Consulted

Alipour, Sam. "Handle with Care." *ESPN The Magazine*, March 22, 2013.

Detroit Free Press. "Tigers' Miguel Cabrera, Justin Verlander Ranked No. 1-2 in ESPN Baseball Tonight's Top 500 Players." March 29, 2013.

Gregory, Sean. "Miguel Cabrera Wins Historic Triple Crown. But Is He the Best Player in Baseball?" *Time*, October 3, 2012.

Miguel Cabrera Foundation: "Major League Baseball Star Miguel Cabrera is Dedicated to Helping Kids Hit a Home Run in Life!" http://www.miguelcabrerafoundation.org/about-miguel-cabrera/

Oakland Press. "Even After a Victory, Leyland Stirs the Pot." April 23, 2008.

Olney, Buster, and Ian Gordon. "Hold On to Miguel Cabrera. The Multitalented Marlin Has Just Begun to Make a Splash." *ESPN The Magazine*, March 15, 2004.

Olney, Buster. "Marlins Close Rocket Age With Dramatic Win." *ESPN The Magazine*, October 22, 2003.

Phillips, Mike. "Cabrera, 16, Shows Off At PPS." *The Miami Herald*, August 5, 1999.

Rodriguez, Juan C. "Crown Prince." *Sun Sentinel*, February 22, 2004.

Sanchez, Jesse. "'Miguelito' No Joke On the Field." MLB.com, March 18, 2005.

Stark, Jayson. "An Incredible Journey for Miguel Cabrera." ESPN.com, March 8, 2013.

On the Internet

Detroit Tigers, MLB Player Stats: "Miguel Cabrera" http://mlb.mlb.com/team/player.jsp?player_id=408234&c_id=det&player_name=Miguel-Cabrera#gameType='R'§ionType=career&statType=1&season=2013&level='ALL'

Detroit Tigers: "Tigers Kids" http://detroit.tigers.mlb.com/det/fan_forum/kids_index.jsp

Miguel Cabrera Foundation http://www.miguelcabrerafoundation.org

GLOSSARY

amateur (AM-uh-chur)—Someone who takes part in a sport or other activity for fun rather than for money.

blood alcohol level (BLUHD AL-kuh-hawl LEV-uhl)—The amount of alcohol in a person's blood after they have been drinking alcohol.

contract (KON-trakt)—A written agreement between two or more people or companies, in which each person or company agrees to do or not do something specific.

counseling (KOUN-suh-ling)—Guidance given to a person to help solve a problem or problems.

foundation (foun-DAY-shuhn)—An organization that supports good causes.

fundamental (fuhn-duh-MEN-tuhl)—Basic, needed for everything else to work properly.

major leagues (MAY-jer LEEGS)—In baseball, the highest level of play in the United States.

minor league (MY-ner LEEG)—In baseball, a series of teams where players play and practice before they are sent to the major leagues.

professional (pruh-FESH-uh-nuhl)—Someone who is paid to do something, often something that others do for fun, like baseball.

RBIs—Runs batted in; the number of runs scored when a player hits the ball.

rookie (ROOHK-ee)—An athlete who is in his or her first season with a professional sports team.

sacrifice (SAK-ruh-fice)—To give up something valuable in order to get something even more valuable.

scouts (SKOUTZ)—People who watch players to see if they are good enough to be signed to a team.

Triple Crown (TRIP-uhl KROUN)—In baseball, an award given to a player whose statistics are the highest in the league in three categories (home runs, RBIs, and batting average) in a single year.

wild-card team (WYELD-kahrd teem)—A team that earns a spot in the playoffs, even though they did not finish with the best record in their division.

INDEX